Freedom of Speech in a Diverse World

C. P. Kumar
Reiki Healer
Roorkee - 247667, India

Disclaimer

While every effort has been made to ensure the accuracy and completeness of the content in this book, the author cannot guarantee that the information contained herein is error-free, up-to-date, or suitable for every individual circumstance.

The author shall not be held liable or responsible for any errors or omissions in the content of the book, nor for any damages, or losses that may arise from any actions taken based upon the suggestions or contents presented in the book.

Readers are advised to use their own judgment and discretion in applying the information provided in this book, and to consult with qualified professionals before taking any action based on the contents of this book. The author disclaims any and all liability or responsibility for any actions taken or not taken based on the information contained in this book.

DEDICATION

To all those who believe in the power of words, and the boundless potential of diverse voices, this book is dedicated to you.

May the pages within reflect the profound significance of a world where Freedom of Speech stands as a cornerstone, where ideas flow freely, and conversations thrive.

In honor of the thinkers, the speakers, the writers, who champion the right to express, challenge, and inspire, may this exploration of "Freedom of Speech in a Diverse World" ignite discussions that transcend borders and barriers.

To the seekers of truth, the advocates of justice, and the defenders of open dialogue, may this compilation of insights shed light on the complexities of safeguarding speech in a global tapestry of perspectives.

As we navigate the historical tapestry of evolving laws, the digital landscapes, and the intricate intersections of culture, religion, and politics, may this volume serve as a compass, guiding us through the nuances of preserving and expanding the freedom that shapes societies.

In recognition of the courageous voices that stir change, and the diligent minds that diligently protect the balance between liberty and responsibility, may the wisdom shared within these chapters remind us that with great freedom comes the even greater duty to uphold truth.

Here's to fostering understanding in a world that thrives on diversity, to embracing the power of words that move minds, and to championing the essential right that empowers us all.

With deepest respect for those who uphold the ideals of freedom, this book is dedicated to the tireless pursuit of unfettered expression, illuminating a path towards a more inclusive and enlightened world.

C. P. Kumar

CONTENTS

PREFACE

In a world that pulsates with diversity, where cultures interweave, ideas collide, and beliefs converge, the concept of freedom of speech stands as both a beacon of human liberty and a complex battleground of ideas. Welcome to a journey that delves into the heart of this dynamic landscape – a journey through the pages of "Freedom of Speech in a Diverse World."

As our societies evolve and interconnect, the age-old notion of freedom of speech takes on new dimensions, intricacies, and challenges. This book is your guide to exploring those dimensions, understanding those intricacies, and confronting those challenges. We invite you to accompany us through a thought-provoking exploration of how the concept of expression, which lies at the core of human progress, navigates the uncharted waters of a modern world.

In the introductory chapter, "Understanding Freedom of Speech in a Modern World," we lay the foundation by examining the philosophical underpinnings of this fundamental right. From there, we embark on a historical odyssey, tracing the Evolution of Freedom of Speech Laws through the ages, revealing how societies have grappled with the balance between liberty and order.

The Role of Media in Promoting or Restricting Freedom of Speech explores the intricate dance between journalism, information dissemination, and societal influence. Moving into the realm of workplaces, we scrutinize how the boundaries of speech extend into professional domains in Freedom of Speech in the Workplace.

In an era defined by diversity, Cultural Sensitivity and Freedom of Speech addresses the challenges of preserving expression while respecting varied worldviews. The intersection of faith and discourse is dissected in The Intersection of Religion and Freedom of Speech, unveiling the intricate tapestry of rights and reverence.

The tension between safeguarding expression and combating hatred takes center stage in Balancing Rights: Freedom of Speech vs. Hate Speech. We then navigate the intriguing space of Defamation and Freedom of Speech, where words wield power, often walking the tightrope between assertion and injury.

The phenomenon of Chilling Effects examines the subtle art of self-censorship, a reaction to the currents of societal norms and pressures. Political Correctness and Freedom of Speech thrusts us into debates about linguistic choices and their implications, revealing the influence of language on thought.

In the digital age, the advent of Social Media has both broadened the avenues for expression and raised new challenges for protecting free discourse. Inevitably, we confront the elephant in the virtual room – Censorship, uncovering its complex motivations, forms, and consequences.

The proliferation of Fake News and Disinformation probes the dark side of expression, where manipulation and deception undermine the very essence of truth. We then delve into the ethical underpinnings of freedom of speech in The Ethics of Freedom of Speech: Rights and Responsibilities.

As pillars of democracy tremble worldwide, we scrutinize The Role of Freedom of Speech in Democracy, examining how the two concepts are inextricably linked. Globalization's intricate dance with expression takes the spotlight in The Influence of Globalization on Freedom of Speech.

Navigating the treacherous terrain of the digital age, we uncover the realm of Freedom of Speech in the Digital Age: Online Activism and Cybersecurity, where unprecedented connectivity births both empowerment and vulnerability.

Finally, as we gaze into the horizon, we confront Future Challenges and Prospects for Freedom of Speech, envisioning the battlegrounds and breakthroughs that await.

"Freedom of Speech in a Diverse World" is a voyage through the crossroads of expression and restraint, freedom and responsibility. Join us on this journey as we unravel the tapestry of speech's complexities and traverse the spectrum of its implications. The pages that follow are a testament to the power of words, the resilience of ideas, and the perpetual quest for the truest form of human liberation.

C. P. Kumar
Reiki Healer
Former Scientist 'G', National Institute of Hydrology
Roorkee - 247667, India
E-mail: cpkumar@yahoo.com
Web: https://www.angelfire.com/nh/cpkumar/virgo.html

Chapter 1. Understanding Freedom of Speech in a Modern World

Introduction

In an increasingly interconnected and diverse world, the concept of freedom of speech holds a central place in discussions of democracy, human rights, and societal progress. As societies evolve and technology reshapes communication, understanding the nuances of freedom of speech becomes paramount. This chapter delves into the multifaceted nature of freedom of speech in the modern context, exploring its significance, limitations, challenges, and potential impacts on diverse societies.

The Significance of Freedom of Speech

1. A Pillar of Democracy

Freedom of speech, often considered a cornerstone of democratic societies, enables citizens to express their opinions, share information, and engage in critical discourse. It empowers individuals to participate in public affairs, fostering transparency, accountability, and informed decision-making. By encouraging diverse viewpoints, freedom of speech contributes to the vibrancy of democratic processes.

2. Facilitating Innovation and Progress

Innovation flourishes in environments where ideas can be freely exchanged. Freedom of speech encourages intellectual exploration, enabling the emergence of new concepts and solutions to societal challenges. Throughout history, groundbreaking advancements in science, technology, and the arts have been fueled by the open exchange of ideas and perspectives.

The Limits of Freedom of Speech

1. Balancing Rights and Responsibilities

While freedom of speech is fundamental, its exercise is not without limitations. The often-cited example of shouting "fire" in a crowded theater highlights the concept of responsible speech. Speech that incites violence, promotes hate, or jeopardizes public safety can be curtailed to protect the well-being of individuals and communities. Balancing individual rights with societal responsibilities is essential to prevent harm.

2. Defamation and Hate Speech

The rise of online communication platforms has magnified the challenges associated with defamation and hate speech. Striking a balance between allowing robust discourse and preventing the spread of harmful misinformation requires thoughtful legal frameworks and community standards. Defining the boundaries of acceptable speech becomes complex in a globalized digital landscape.

Challenges in the Modern Context

1. Digital Transformation and Global Reach

The digital age has revolutionized communication, offering unprecedented reach and immediacy. However, this transformation has also brought challenges. Online spaces can become breeding grounds for misinformation, echo chambers, and toxic behavior. The borderless nature of the internet complicates regulatory efforts, necessitating international cooperation to address digital challenges to freedom of speech.

2. Filter Bubbles and Echo Chambers

As algorithms tailor content to individual preferences, users are often exposed to information that reinforces their existing beliefs—a phenomenon known as the filter bubble. This can lead to echo chambers, where diverse perspectives are excluded, and extreme views are amplified. Overcoming this challenge requires media literacy education and designing platforms that expose users to a wider range of viewpoints.

Navigating Cultural Sensitivities

1. Cultural Relativism and Universal Rights

The clash between cultural sensitivities and freedom of speech is a complex issue. Different cultures hold varying norms and values regarding acceptable expression. While freedom of speech is a universal human right, its interpretation can vary. Striking a balance between respecting cultural diversity and upholding fundamental rights requires open dialogue and mutual understanding.

2. Addressing Blasphemy and Taboos

Speech that is considered blasphemous or taboo in one culture may be protected expression in another. The tension between freedom of speech and religious or cultural beliefs can lead to conflicts. Navigating these issues involves recognizing the importance of respectful dialogue and finding common ground that respects individual rights while promoting social cohesion.

The Impact on Diverse Societies

1. Empowerment of Marginalized Voices

Freedom of speech can be a powerful tool for marginalized groups to challenge systemic injustices and advocate for their rights. Social media and digital platforms provide spaces for individuals who have historically been silenced to amplify their voices and share their experiences. However, these platforms also need to address harassment and ensure equitable representation.

2. Managing Disinformation and Fake News

The spread of disinformation and fake news poses a significant threat to democratic discourse. Manipulative actors can exploit the open nature of communication to disseminate false information, undermining trust in institutions and eroding the credibility of accurate reporting. Strengthening media literacy efforts and promoting responsible journalism are essential to combating this challenge.

Conclusion

In a rapidly changing world, understanding freedom of speech requires a nuanced approach that considers its significance, limitations, challenges, and impact on diverse societies. While it remains a foundational pillar of democracy, its application must be tempered with a sense of responsibility. The digital age brings both opportunities and perils, necessitating a delicate balance between facilitating open discourse and safeguarding against harm. Navigating cultural sensitivities requires an appreciation for the complex interplay between universal rights and local norms. Ultimately, ensuring the health of modern societies requires ongoing dialogue, education, and adaptation to address the evolving landscape of freedom of speech.

Introduction

The concept of freedom of speech is a cornerstone of democratic societies, allowing individuals to express their thoughts, ideas, and opinions without fear of censorship or reprisal. However, the journey toward establishing and safeguarding this fundamental right has been a long and complex one, shaped by historical, cultural, and legal developments. This chapter explores the evolution of freedom of speech laws, tracing their origins from ancient civilizations to the modern era, and highlighting the challenges and triumphs along the way.

Early Civilizations and Oral Tradition

The history of freedom of speech can be traced back to ancient civilizations where oral communication was the primary means of expression. In societies like ancient Greece and Rome, citizens engaged in public discourse in the form of speeches, debates, and theatrical performances. While not always an absolute right, these societies laid the groundwork for valuing open expression and debate.

Medieval and Renaissance Periods

1. Era of Ecclesiastical Control

The medieval period witnessed the dominance of religious institutions and monarchies, often leading to suppression of dissenting voices. The Catholic Church wielded considerable power, censoring works it deemed heretical or blasphemous. However, amidst these constraints, early thinkers like John Wycliffe and Jan Hus advocated for individual conscience and criticized ecclesiastical authority.

2. Rise of Printing Press

The Renaissance marked a turning point with the invention of the printing press, allowing ideas to spread more widely. Figures like Martin Luther challenged religious orthodoxy, leading to significant debates on matters of faith and governance. The printing press played a pivotal role in the emergence of a more diverse range of voices, laying the groundwork for the modern concept of freedom of speech.

Enlightenment and Emergence of Modern Liberties

1. Philosophical Foundations

The Enlightenment era of the 17th and 18th centuries saw the crystallization of ideas about individual rights and freedoms. Thinkers like John Locke and Voltaire championed the notion of free expression as essential for a just society. Their writings laid the intellectual groundwork for the future development of legal protections for freedom of speech.

2. American and French Revolutions

The American Revolution in 1776 and the French Revolution in 1789 marked critical moments in the evolution of freedom of speech laws. Documents like the United States Constitution's First Amendment and the French Declaration of the Rights of Man and of the Citizen enshrined the right to express one's opinions without fear of censorship. These developments marked the formal recognition of freedom of speech as a fundamental human right.

19th Century: Balancing Acts and Legal Frameworks

1. Emergence of Legal Precedents

The 19th century saw the gradual establishment of legal frameworks for freedom of speech. Landmark cases like the 1832 trial of the British reformer Richard Carlile and the U.S. Supreme Court case of Schenck v. United States in 1919 defined the boundaries of free speech. The famous phrase "clear and present danger" emerged from the latter case, acknowledging that speech could be restricted if it posed an imminent threat to public safety.

2. Challenges and Progress

The 19th century also posed challenges to the growing concept of free expression. Governments often struggled to strike a balance between preserving order and protecting individual liberties. Despite setbacks, movements like the abolitionist movement, suffragette movement, and labor rights activism relied heavily on freedom of speech to advocate for change.

20th Century: Tests and Expansions

1. World Wars and Free Speech

The 20th century was marked by two World Wars that strained the limits of freedom of speech. Governments invoked national security concerns to curtail dissenting voices, leading to instances of censorship and suppression. The landmark U.S. Supreme Court case of Brandenburg v. Ohio in 1969, however, reinforced the importance of protecting even offensive speech unless it incited immediate lawless action.

The mid-20th century witnessed the civil rights movement, which harnessed the power of speech and assembly to challenge racial discrimination. Figures like Martin Luther King Jr. eloquently articulated the demand for equal rights, showcasing the transformative potential of free expression. Additionally, the counterculture movements of the 1960s challenged societal norms and pushed the boundaries of creative expression.

21st Century: Digital Age and New Challenges

1. Internet and Global Connectivity

The 21st century ushered in the digital age, transforming the landscape of free speech. The internet provided a platform for unprecedented global communication, enabling individuals to share their thoughts instantaneously. However, this digital realm also posed new challenges, including the spread of hate speech, misinformation, and cyberbullying.

2. Balancing Rights in the Digital Era

As societies grapple with the implications of digital communication, the balance between free speech and other rights, such as privacy and security, has become more complex. The rise of social media platforms has forced legal systems to adapt to new forms of expression and potential harms. Countries around the world are exploring how to regulate online speech without stifling legitimate discourse.

Conclusion

The evolution of freedom of speech laws has been a dynamic journey, reflecting the changing nature of societies and the values they hold dear. From the oral traditions of ancient civilizations to the digital landscapes of the modern era, the fight for free expression has seen both triumphs and setbacks. As we navigate the complexities of a diverse world, it's crucial to strike a balance that protects this fundamental right while acknowledging the responsibilities that come with it. Only by nurturing a diverse ecosystem of expression can we ensure that the voices of all individuals are heard, contributing to the vibrant tapestry of global discourse.

Introduction

In a rapidly evolving and interconnected world, the concept of freedom of speech holds a pivotal position, serving as a cornerstone of democratic societies. The ability to express thoughts, opinions, and ideas without fear of censorship or retribution is a fundamental human right, ensuring an open exchange of diverse perspectives. One of the critical actors in shaping the landscape of freedom of speech is the media. The media, encompassing various platforms such as traditional newspapers, television, radio, and the internet, wields immense influence over public discourse. However, this influence comes with a dual nature, as media can either serve as a champion of free expression or as a harbinger of restriction. This chapter delves into the multifaceted role of media in promoting or restricting freedom of speech within the context of a diverse world.

The Power of Media in Shaping Public Discourse

1. The Information Gatekeepers

Media acts as the primary channel through which information flows within societies. It plays a crucial role in informing the public about current events, political developments, social issues, and cultural happenings. As information gatekeepers, media outlets have the responsibility to ensure that diverse perspectives are represented accurately, enabling citizens to make informed decisions. This role is especially significant in diverse societies, where differing viewpoints and experiences contribute to a rich tapestry of ideas.

2. Media as a Catalyst for Social Change

Historically, media has been a driving force behind social change. Through investigative journalism, documentaries, and exposés, media can expose injustices, corruption, and human rights violations, prompting public outrage and calls for reform. Media's role in amplifying marginalized voices has been pivotal in promoting social equality and justice. In diverse societies, media can highlight the stories of underrepresented communities, fostering empathy and understanding among different groups.

Promoting Freedom of Speech

1. Facilitating Open Dialogue

Media, when functioning optimally, serves as a platform for open dialogue and debate. It provides a space where individuals from various backgrounds can share their perspectives, challenge prevailing narratives, and engage in constructive discussions. This diversity of viewpoints is essential for fostering critical thinking and a well-rounded understanding of complex issues.

2. Media Pluralism and Diverse Voices

Media pluralism, the presence of a variety of media outlets with diverse ownership, is essential for safeguarding freedom of speech. In a diverse world, media outlets that cater to different languages, cultures, and viewpoints allow citizens to access information that resonates with their identities and experiences. This not only empowers marginalized groups but also contributes to a more comprehensive understanding of global events.

3. Role of Digital Media

The rise of digital media, particularly social media platforms, has revolutionized the way information is disseminated and consumed. These platforms have democratized the process of sharing opinions, allowing individuals to express themselves on a global scale. Digital media's interactive nature encourages participation, facilitating grassroots movements, and enabling citizens to hold institutions accountable.

Restricting Freedom of Speech

1. The Challenge of Misinformation

While media has the potential to promote freedom of speech, it also faces significant challenges, chief among them being the spread of misinformation. The rapid dissemination of false or misleading information can erode public trust and create an environment where informed discourse becomes difficult. In diverse societies, misinformation can exploit existing divisions and amplify prejudices, thereby restricting open dialogue.

2. Sensationalism and Polarization

Media outlets seeking higher viewership or readership often resort to sensationalism, focusing on emotionally charged stories rather than substantive issues. This tendency can lead to the polarization of society, as news coverage becomes increasingly biased and sensationalized. In diverse communities, sensationalist reporting can reinforce stereotypes and hinder meaningful cross-cultural understanding.

3. The Threat of Digital Echo Chambers

While digital media offers a platform for diverse voices, it can paradoxically contribute to the formation of echo chambers—online spaces where individuals are exposed only to viewpoints that align with their existing beliefs. This isolation from diverse perspectives can reinforce preconceived notions, discourage critical thinking, and lead to a narrowing of the ideological landscape.

Media Ethics and Responsibility

1. Balancing Freedom and Responsibility

The media's role in promoting or restricting freedom of speech hinges on its ethical standards and sense of responsibility. Journalistic integrity requires a delicate balance between the freedom to report on issues of public interest and the responsibility to ensure accuracy, fairness, and respect for individual rights. In a diverse world, this balance becomes even more critical, as media outlets must navigate the complexities of cultural sensitivities.

2. The Role of Editorial Independence

Editorial independence, the ability of media outlets to operate without undue influence from external actors, is paramount for upholding freedom of speech. Media organizations that prioritize editorial independence can resist pressures to conform to certain narratives or biases, thus fostering a more open and diverse media landscape.

Government Regulation and Media Freedom

Governments often grapple with the question of how much regulation is necessary to ensure responsible media practices without infringing on freedom of speech. While certain regulations, such as those combating hate speech or incitement to violence, may be necessary to maintain social harmony, overly restrictive measures can stifle open discourse and freedom of expression. Striking the right balance is a complex task, particularly in societies with diverse cultural norms and values.

Conclusion

In a diverse world, the role of media in promoting or restricting freedom of speech is a complex interplay of power, responsibility, and ethics. Media's ability to facilitate open dialogue, amplify marginalized voices, and expose injustices underscores its potential as a champion of free expression. However, the challenges of misinformation, sensationalism, and digital echo chambers remind us of the delicate balance between media's positive contributions and its potential to curtail free speech. As societies continue to navigate the complexities of diversity, media outlets, regulators, and consumers must collectively strive to uphold the principles of freedom of speech while fostering a respectful and inclusive public discourse.

Introduction

In today's diverse and interconnected world, the concept of freedom of speech has evolved to encompass a myriad of contexts, including the workplace. The workplace, once thought of as a space solely dedicated to professional pursuits, has now become a microcosm of societal values, opinions, and expressions. However, the intersection of freedom of speech and the workplace presents a complex challenge, as it necessitates a delicate balance between individual expression and the need for maintaining a respectful and productive environment. This chapter delves into the multifaceted dimensions of freedom of speech in the workplace, exploring its implications, limitations, and potential resolutions.

The Foundations of Freedom of Speech

Before delving into the intricacies of freedom of speech in the workplace, it's essential to revisit the foundational principles that underpin this fundamental right. Freedom of speech, a cornerstone of democratic societies, empowers individuals to express their thoughts, opinions, and ideas without fear of censorship or retaliation. This right is enshrined in various international conventions and national constitutions, emphasizing its significance in promoting the exchange of diverse viewpoints and fostering a vibrant public discourse.

The Shifting Landscape of the Workplace

The modern workplace, characterized by its diverse workforce and emphasis on inclusivity, is a reflection of the broader society. With globalization and advancements in communication technology, workplaces have become melting pots of cultures, beliefs, and perspectives. This diversity brings richness to the working environment but also poses challenges when reconciling differing viewpoints, especially when they touch on sensitive subjects.

Balancing Freedom of Speech and Workplace Harmony

1. The Paradox of Expression and Respect

While freedom of speech encourages open dialogue, it can clash with the necessity of maintaining a harmonious and respectful workplace. What might be seen as a legitimate expression of personal opinion by one individual could be deeply offensive or discriminatory to another. Employers and employees alike grapple with the question of how to foster an environment where freedom of speech is respected while ensuring that expressions do not infringe upon the rights or dignity of others.

2. The Role of Employers in Setting Boundaries

Employers have a pivotal role in defining the boundaries of acceptable speech within the workplace. Crafting and enforcing clear codes of conduct and anti-discrimination policies helps establish a framework for healthy dialogue while curbing harmful expressions. However, finding the balance between safeguarding employee well-being and preserving individual freedom of speech requires a nuanced approach.

Navigating Sensitive Topics

1. Political and Social Discourse

In an era marked by intense political polarization and social activism, conversations surrounding politics and social issues can easily spill into the workplace. While individuals have the right to express their views, employers must remain vigilant to prevent discussions from turning into divisive debates that disrupt the work environment. Encouraging constructive conversations that emphasize understanding rather than persuasion can help create an atmosphere where diverse opinions coexist peacefully.

2. Religion and Cultural Sensitivities

Religious beliefs and cultural practices often influence personal identities, and discussing them can be deeply meaningful. However, these discussions also have the potential to offend or alienate colleagues who hold differing beliefs. Organizations must prioritize inclusivity and sensitivity, allowing employees to share their cultural and religious perspectives in ways that educate and enlighten, rather than marginalize.

The Role of Technology and Social Media

1. The Blurring of Personal and Professional Spheres

The advent of social media has blurred the lines between personal and professional lives, allowing individuals to express themselves beyond the confines of the workplace. However, these online expressions can have real-world implications, affecting an individual's professional reputation and the reputation of the organization. It is incumbent upon both employees and employers to be mindful of the potential consequences of their online speech.

The digital realm has brought about new challenges, including the rise of online harassment and cyberbullying. These issues can seep into the workplace, creating a hostile and uncomfortable environment for targeted individuals. Organizations must establish guidelines for online conduct and provide resources for reporting and addressing instances of harassment.

Fostering Constructive Dialogue and Inclusion

1. Promoting Active Listening

One way to navigate the delicate balance between freedom of speech and a harmonious workplace is by promoting active listening. Encouraging individuals to genuinely understand the viewpoints of others before responding fosters empathy and diffuses potential conflicts. Training programs that focus on effective communication skills can contribute to creating an environment of respectful dialogue.

2. Educating for Awareness

Educational initiatives that promote cultural awareness, diversity, and inclusion can facilitate meaningful interactions among employees. When individuals understand the historical and cultural contexts that shape different perspectives, they are more likely to engage in informed and respectful conversations.

Conclusion

Freedom of speech in the workplace is a dynamic and complex issue that requires careful consideration and deliberate action. While this fundamental right is integral to maintaining democratic values, it must be navigated with a sense of responsibility and respect for others. By fostering an environment that encourages open dialogue, active listening, and cultural awareness, organizations can strike a balance between individual expression and the harmonious functioning of the workplace. In a world that continues to grow more diverse and interconnected, the ability to engage in constructive conversations while upholding the dignity of all individuals remains an essential skill for every member of the workforce.

Introduction

Freedom of speech is a fundamental human right that has been at the core of democratic societies for centuries. It allows individuals to express their ideas, opinions, and beliefs without fear of censorship or punishment. However, the concept of freedom of speech becomes complex and nuanced when it intersects with cultural sensitivity. In an increasingly diverse world, where people from different backgrounds, cultures, and belief systems coexist, striking a balance between the exercise of free speech and the avoidance of cultural insensitivity is a challenge that demands careful consideration. This chapter delves into the intricate relationship between cultural sensitivity and freedom of speech, exploring the tensions, implications, and potential solutions that arise when these two principles collide.

The Foundation of Freedom of Speech

1. Historical Roots and Importance

Freedom of speech has its origins in the Enlightenment era, when philosophers and thinkers championed the idea that individuals should be able to express their thoughts and ideas without fear of persecution. The concept gained prominence in documents such as the United States' First Amendment and the Universal Declaration of Human Rights, solidifying its status as a fundamental human right. The principle serves as a cornerstone of democracy, enabling citizens to engage in public discourse, criticize authority, and contribute to the development of society.

2. The Challenge of Cultural Sensitivity

Defining Cultural Sensitivity

Cultural sensitivity refers to the awareness, understanding, and respect for different cultural norms, practices, and beliefs. It recognizes the diversity that exists within society and seeks to avoid actions or expressions that may marginalize, offend, or disrespect individuals or groups based on their cultural backgrounds.

The Clash of Values

While freedom of speech advocates for open and unrestricted expression, cultural sensitivity emphasizes the importance of avoiding harm and promoting inclusivity. These two values can sometimes come into conflict when speech that is protected as a right is deemed offensive or hurtful to certain cultural or ethnic groups. Balancing the preservation of free expression with the responsibility to prevent harm is a delicate task.

Navigating the Tensions

1. The Paradox of Tolerance

Philosopher Karl Popper introduced the "paradox of tolerance," which highlights the dilemma of how to deal with intolerant speech in a tolerant society. If a society becomes overly permissive and allows hate speech or discriminatory rhetoric to go unchecked, it may end up undermining the very values it seeks to protect. Striking a balance between preserving freedom of speech and preventing the spread of harmful ideologies is a complex challenge.

2. The Role of Context

Context plays a crucial role in assessing the potential impact of speech on cultural sensitivity. What might be acceptable within one context or cultural group could be deeply offensive in another. Recognizing these nuances is essential for fostering meaningful conversations while minimizing harm.

3. Responsibility and Accountability

While freedom of speech provides individuals with the right to express their opinions, it also entails a responsibility to consider the potential consequences of their words. Holding individuals accountable for their speech, particularly when it crosses the line into hate speech or incitement to violence, is essential for maintaining a healthy discourse and protecting vulnerable communities.

Implications for a Diverse Society

1. Marginalization and Exclusion

Insensitive speech can lead to the marginalization and exclusion of minority groups, further deepening societal divides. When individuals from marginalized communities are subjected to derogatory or disrespectful language, their ability to participate in public discourse and civic life can be compromised.

2. Impact on Social Cohesion

Cultural insensitivity has the potential to erode social cohesion by creating tension and mistrust among different cultural and ethnic groups. A society that values diversity and inclusivity must find ways to ensure that all members feel respected and heard.

Fostering Cultural Sensitivity

1. Education and Awareness

Promoting cultural sensitivity begins with education and awareness. Schools, workplaces, and community organizations can play a crucial role in fostering understanding and respect for different cultures, beliefs, and perspectives.

2. Dialogue and Constructive Discourse

Engaging in open and constructive dialogue allows individuals from various backgrounds to share their experiences and perspectives. This can lead to greater empathy and a deeper understanding of the challenges faced by different cultural groups.

3. Media Responsibility

Media outlets have a significant impact on shaping public opinion and cultural attitudes. Responsible journalism and media practices involve considering the potential consequences of the content they produce, striving to avoid perpetuating stereotypes or promoting discriminatory narratives.

Conclusion

The intersection of cultural sensitivity and freedom of speech poses a complex dilemma in our diverse world. While the right to express oneself freely is a cornerstone of democratic societies, it must be exercised responsibly to avoid causing harm to marginalized or vulnerable groups. Striking a balance between these principles requires nuanced approaches that take into account context, accountability, and the broader social implications of speech. By fostering cultural sensitivity, promoting dialogue, and encouraging responsible media practices, societies can navigate these tensions while nurturing inclusivity, respect, and a thriving democratic discourse. In embracing both freedom of speech and cultural sensitivity, we can create a more harmonious and equitable global community.

Introduction

Freedom of speech is a fundamental human right that plays a crucial role in modern democratic societies. It allows individuals to express their thoughts, ideas, and opinions without fear of censorship or persecution. However, the exercise of this right becomes complex when it intersects with religious beliefs and sensitivities. The delicate balance between freedom of speech and respect for religious convictions has been a topic of ongoing debate, raising questions about the boundaries of expression and the potential consequences of offending religious sensibilities. This chapter delves into the intricate relationship between religion and freedom of speech, examining various perspectives, challenges, and potential solutions.

Understanding Freedom of Speech and Religion

1. Defining Freedom of Speech

Freedom of speech, often considered a cornerstone of democratic societies, encompasses the right to express one's thoughts, ideas, opinions, and beliefs through various forms of communication. This right is enshrined in international human rights documents, such as the Universal Declaration of Human Rights, which recognizes the importance of fostering open discourse and protecting individuals from state-imposed censorship.

2. The Significance of Religious Beliefs

Religion holds deep significance for many individuals and communities. It informs their values, provides a sense of identity, and guides their moral compass. Religious beliefs often shape individuals' worldviews and influence their understanding of what is sacred and inviolable. As a result, the clash between freedom of speech and religious convictions can give rise to complex ethical and legal dilemmas.

Freedom of Speech and Religious Sensitivities

1. The Right to Offend vs. Respect for Beliefs

One of the central challenges in this intersection is finding a balance between the right to express potentially offensive or controversial ideas and the duty to respect religious beliefs. Advocates of an expansive view of freedom of speech argue that no idea or belief should be immune to criticism or satire, including religious ones. They stress that a society's progress depends on the ability to question and challenge prevailing norms, including religious dogmas.

On the other hand, proponents of limiting speech in the context of religion emphasize the importance of protecting individuals from harm, including emotional distress and incitement to violence. They argue that certain forms of speech can perpetuate stereotypes, stoke hatred, and lead to discrimination against religious groups. The challenge lies in determining when speech crosses the line from legitimate critique to harmful provocation.

The impact of speech on religious sentiments can vary greatly depending on cultural and religious context. What may be considered acceptable criticism in one culture might be deeply offensive in another. Therefore, a nuanced understanding of the context in which speech occurs is essential when assessing its potential consequences. This calls for a more inclusive and culturally sensitive approach to analyzing speech that intersects with religious beliefs.

Legal Frameworks and Case Studies

1. International Legal Perspectives

Different legal systems around the world approach the balance between freedom of speech and religious sensitivity differently. In the United States, for instance, the First Amendment of the Constitution guarantees robust protection of free speech, even if it involves criticism of religion. In contrast, some European countries have enacted laws that criminalize hate speech and incitement to religious hatred, reflecting a more balanced approach between speech and societal harmony.

2. Case Study: The Danish Cartoon Controversy

The Danish cartoon controversy, which emerged in 2005 after the publication of caricatures depicting the Prophet Muhammad in a Danish newspaper, underscored the global nature of the intersection between religion and freedom of speech. The cartoons led to widespread protests and calls for boycotts across the Muslim world, highlighting the potential for speech to inflame religious tensions on an international scale. The incident prompted discussions about cultural sensitivity, journalistic responsibility, and the limits of satire.

3. Case Study: The Charlie Hebdo Attack

The tragic attack on the French satirical magazine Charlie Hebdo in 2015 highlighted the complexities of the freedom of speech and religion debate. The magazine had a history of publishing cartoons that many Muslims found offensive and blasphemous. The attack sparked discussions about the limits of free expression, the role of cultural sensitivity, and the responsibilities of both creators and consumers of speech.

Fostering Dialogue and Mutual Respect

1. Education and Interfaith Communication

One way to address the tensions between freedom of speech and religious beliefs is through education and interfaith communication. Promoting understanding and dialogue between individuals from diverse religious backgrounds can help dispel misconceptions and reduce the likelihood of offense. Education can encourage critical thinking while also fostering empathy and respect for differing perspectives.

2. Media Responsibility and Ethical Reporting

Media outlets play a significant role in shaping public discourse, including discussions about religion. Responsible journalism entails a commitment to accuracy, fairness, and sensitivity. Media professionals can contribute to the constructive exchange of ideas by avoiding sensationalism and carefully considering the potential impact of their content on religious communities.

Conclusion

The intersection of religion and freedom of speech is a multifaceted issue that demands thoughtful consideration. While the right to express ideas and beliefs is essential for the progress of society, it is equally important to respect the deeply held convictions of individuals and communities. Achieving this delicate balance requires open dialogue, cultural understanding, and a willingness to challenge our own preconceptions. By fostering an environment where freedom of speech coexists harmoniously with respect for religious beliefs, we can strive towards a more inclusive and diverse world that values both expression and empathy.

Introduction

In a diverse and interconnected world, the concept of freedom of speech is both a fundamental human right and a complex ethical challenge. While the freedom to express one's thoughts and opinions is crucial for the functioning of democratic societies and the progress of human knowledge, the line between protected speech and harmful speech is not always clear. This chapter explores the delicate balance between freedom of speech and hate speech, delving into the challenges, implications, and potential solutions that arise when these rights intersect.

Defining Freedom of Speech and Hate Speech

1. Freedom of Speech: A Pillar of Democracy

Freedom of speech, often enshrined in constitutions and international declarations, is a cornerstone of democratic societies. It allows individuals to openly express their thoughts, share ideas, and engage in public discourse without fear of censorship or retaliation. This right empowers citizens to participate in shaping public policies, holding governments accountable, and fostering a diverse marketplace of ideas.

2. Identifying Hate Speech

Hate speech, on the other hand, refers to speech, conduct, writing, or expressions that incite violence, discrimination, or hostility against individuals or groups based on attributes such as race, religion, ethnicity, gender, or sexual orientation. While definitions may vary across jurisdictions and cultural contexts, hate speech generally goes beyond the boundaries of acceptable discourse, causing harm and perpetuating systemic inequalities.

Balancing Rights and Protecting Vulnerable Communities

1. The Harm Principle

The "harm principle," introduced by philosopher John Stuart Mill, suggests that the only legitimate reason to limit individual freedoms is to prevent harm to others. When applied to the realm of speech, this principle raises questions about whether hate speech qualifies as harmful and whether its restriction is justified to protect marginalized communities from psychological and physical harm.

2. Strengthening Democracy vs. Preserving Equality

The tension between freedom of speech and the need to prevent harm becomes particularly pronounced when considering the impact of hate speech on marginalized communities. While free expression is vital for a thriving democracy, unchecked hate speech can silence voices, perpetuate discrimination, and undermine the very democratic values that freedom of speech seeks to uphold.

The Role of Digital Platforms

1. The Rise of Online Expression

The advent of digital platforms has revolutionized the way people communicate and exercise their freedom of speech. Social media, blogs, and forums provide global audiences with unprecedented access to a multitude of perspectives. However, this democratization of expression has also given rise to challenges related to hate speech.

2. Content Moderation and the Dilemma of Censorship

Digital platforms often find themselves at the center of the debate over hate speech. On one hand, content moderation is essential to prevent the spread of harmful content and create safe online spaces. On the other hand, concerns about overreach and potential censorship loom large, raising questions about who gets to decide what constitutes hate speech and where to draw the line.

International Perspectives on Hate Speech Regulation

1. Legal Approaches Across Nations

Different countries employ various legal frameworks to address hate speech. Some nations, like the United States, prioritize the protection of even offensive speech under the First Amendment. Contrastingly, several European countries have enacted laws that criminalize hate speech, aiming to curb the incitement of violence and discrimination.

2. The Role of International Organizations

International organizations such as the United Nations have recognized the global significance of addressing hate speech. Initiatives like the Rabat Plan of Action emphasize the importance of finding a balance between freedom of expression and preventing hate speech, promoting dialogue and education as tools to counter intolerance.

Strategies for Balancing Rights

1. Promoting Digital Literacy and Media Literacy

Educational initiatives can play a crucial role in mitigating the impact of hate speech. By promoting digital literacy and media literacy, individuals can develop critical thinking skills, enabling them to distinguish between credible information and harmful propaganda.

2. Encouraging Counter-Speech and Dialogue

Encouraging counter-speech that challenges hate speech narratives can be an effective strategy. When individuals, communities, and organizations unite against hate speech, they send a powerful message that intolerance will not be tolerated. Dialogue platforms that bring together diverse perspectives can also foster understanding and empathy.

3. Transparent and Consistent Content Moderation

Digital platforms should prioritize transparent and consistent content moderation policies. By involving a diverse range of voices in the decision-making process and openly communicating the rationale behind content removal, platforms can build trust and legitimacy while avoiding accusations of bias.

Conclusion

In a diverse world where conflicting rights intersect, the challenge of balancing freedom of speech and hate speech regulation remains complex. The importance of free expression cannot be understated, but neither can the harm caused by hate speech. Achieving the delicate equilibrium between these rights requires careful consideration, collaboration, and a commitment to fostering an inclusive and respectful discourse that empowers individuals without marginalizing or endangering vulnerable communities. As we navigate this landscape, it is essential to remember that protecting human dignity and promoting a society built on justice and equality are goals worth pursuing, even in the face of difficult trade-offs.

Introduction

Freedom of speech is a fundamental right that lies at the heart of democratic societies. It allows individuals to express their thoughts, opinions, and ideas without fear of censorship or reprisal. However, this cherished freedom is not without its limitations, one of the most significant being the concept of defamation. Defamation involves making false statements that harm the reputation of an individual, business, or organization. Balancing the right to free speech with the need to protect individuals from false and damaging statements is a complex challenge that requires careful consideration. This chapter explores the delicate equilibrium between defamation and freedom of speech in a diverse world, examining legal frameworks, landmark cases, and the evolving digital landscape.

Defamation: Understanding the Basics

Defamation refers to the act of making false statements about someone that harm their reputation. These statements can be either spoken (slander) or written (libel). The key elements of defamation typically include:

1. False Statement

For a statement to be defamatory, it must be false. Truth is an absolute defense against defamation claims. Accurate statements, no matter how damaging, cannot be classified as defamatory.

2. Harm to Reputation

The false statement must have the potential to harm the reputation of the individual or entity involved. This harm may manifest as damage to their personal, professional, or social standing.

3. Publication

The false statement must be communicated to a third party, essentially making it public. This distinguishes defamation from mere private conversations.

4. Negligence or Intent

In some legal systems, the plaintiff must demonstrate that the defendant acted either negligently or with intent to harm. Negligence implies that the defendant failed to exercise reasonable care in verifying the accuracy of the statement.

The Interplay with Freedom of Speech

While freedom of speech is a cornerstone of democratic societies, it is not an absolute right. The law recognizes that certain limitations are necessary to prevent the abuse of this freedom, and defamation is one such limitation. The challenge lies in finding the right balance between allowing individuals to express their opinions and protecting individuals from unjustified harm to their reputation.

1. Protecting Individuals and Reputation

Defamation laws serve as safeguards against baseless attacks on individuals' reputations. Without these protections, false and damaging statements could run rampant, causing irreparable harm to individuals' personal and professional lives.

At the same time, robust public discourse is crucial for a vibrant democracy. People must be able to openly discuss matters of public interest without fear of legal reprisal. This is particularly important when discussing matters of political, social, or economic significance.

Landmark Cases

Several landmark cases have played a pivotal role in shaping the boundaries between defamation and freedom of speech. These cases have provided legal precedents and principles that guide courts and legislatures in addressing defamation claims.

1. New York Times Co. v. Sullivan (1964)

In this landmark U.S. Supreme Court case, the court held that public officials must prove "actual malice" on the part of the defendant to establish a defamation claim. This means that the statement was made with knowledge of its falsity or with reckless disregard for the truth. This standard protects robust public debate and ensures that public figures cannot easily stifle criticism through defamation claims.

2. Reynolds v. Times Newspapers Ltd (1999)

In the UK, this case established the "Reynolds Defense," which provides protection to media outlets that publish defamatory statements if they can show that the publication was responsible and in the public interest. This case emphasized the importance of balancing the right to reputation with the public's right to know.

3. Gutnick v. Dow Jones & Company Inc. (2002)

This case highlighted the challenges posed by the internet and cross-border defamation. The Australian High Court ruled that a defamation claim could be brought in Australia against a U.S.-based company for an article published online. This decision demonstrated the global reach of defamation laws and the need to consider jurisdictional issues in the digital age.

The Digital Landscape

The advent of the internet and social media has revolutionized the way information is disseminated, posing new challenges and opportunities in the realm of defamation and freedom of speech.

1. Rapid Spread of Information

The speed at which information can spread online amplifies the potential harm caused by defamatory statements. A false statement can go viral within minutes, causing widespread damage before any corrective action can be taken.

2. Anonymity and Accountability

Online platforms provide a degree of anonymity that can encourage the spread of false and damaging statements. Holding anonymous individuals accountable for defamation can be difficult, raising questions about the practicality of enforcing defamation laws in the digital age.

The borderless nature of the internet raises complex questions about jurisdiction. A defamatory statement made in one country can be accessed and disseminated in another. This challenges traditional notions of jurisdiction and calls for international cooperation in addressing cross-border defamation cases.

Striking the Balance

As technology continues to evolve, so must the legal frameworks that govern defamation and freedom of speech. Striking the right balance between these two fundamental rights requires careful consideration of the complexities of the modern world.

1. Defamation Law Reform

Many legal systems are reevaluating and updating their defamation laws to account for the digital landscape. Balancing the right to reputation with the principles of free expression requires crafting laws that discourage baseless defamation claims while still protecting legitimate criticism and public discourse.

2. Online Content Moderation

Online platforms play a significant role in shaping public discourse. Stricter content moderation policies can help prevent the spread of false and defamatory statements. However, implementing these policies without infringing on legitimate speech remains a challenge.

Given the global nature of the internet, international collaboration is crucial in addressing cross-border defamation cases. Harmonizing legal standards and establishing mechanisms for cooperation can help ensure that individuals are protected from defamation regardless of their geographical location.

Conclusion

The relationship between defamation and freedom of speech is a delicate one, requiring a nuanced understanding of the rights and responsibilities involved. While freedom of speech is a fundamental pillar of democracy, it must be exercised responsibly, recognizing that false and damaging statements can have far-reaching consequences. The evolution of technology and communication platforms presents both challenges and opportunities in navigating this complex landscape. As societies continue to grapple with these issues, the aim should be to strike a balance that upholds the principles of free expression while safeguarding individuals from unwarranted harm to their reputation. In a diverse world, the pursuit of this equilibrium remains an ongoing endeavor.

Introduction

Freedom of speech is a fundamental pillar of democratic societies, allowing individuals to express their thoughts, opinions, and ideas without fear of censorship or reprisal. However, in the complex landscape of a diverse world, this cherished right can sometimes face challenges in the form of "chilling effects," where individuals choose to self-censor out of fear of potential consequences. This chapter explores the phenomenon of chilling effects on freedom of speech, delving into its causes, implications, and potential solutions.

Understanding Chilling Effects

1. Defining Chilling Effects

Chilling effects refer to the suppression or curtailment of speech that occurs when individuals refrain from expressing themselves due to fear of adverse consequences. These consequences might include legal repercussions, social backlash, professional harm, or even threats to personal safety. While the law might protect individuals from direct government censorship, chilling effects highlight the subtler ways in which the freedom of speech can be undermined.

2. Psychological and Societal Factors

Chilling effects are often rooted in psychological and societal factors. Individuals might fear public humiliation, ostracization, or backlash from their communities if their views deviate from prevailing norms. This fear can lead to self-censorship as people opt for silence rather than risking potential harm. Additionally, social media and online platforms can amplify these effects, as the potential for viral outrage or targeted harassment becomes a real concern.

The Role of Technology and Online Platforms

1. Amplification of Chilling Effects

The digital age has introduced new dimensions to chilling effects. Online platforms, while offering a global stage for expression, can also become breeding grounds for hostility and vitriol. The perceived permanence of online content and the ease of sharing can intensify fears of backlash, leading individuals to carefully curate their online presence or even avoid certain topics altogether.

2. Algorithmic Bias and Echo Chambers

Algorithmic bias within social media algorithms can also contribute to chilling effects. Recommendation algorithms that prioritize content similar to what users have engaged with before can create echo chambers, reinforcing existing beliefs and deterring users from exploring diverse perspectives. This narrowing of exposure can discourage individuals from expressing dissenting views, perpetuating self-censorship.

Consequences of Chilling Effects

1. Erosion of Pluralism

Chilling effects can erode the pluralism that is crucial for healthy democratic discourse. When individuals are hesitant to voice minority opinions or challenge prevailing narratives, the public discourse becomes skewed and less representative of the diverse range of perspectives within a society. This erosion of pluralism can lead to a less informed citizenry and the perpetuation of misinformation.

2. Impact on Creativity and Innovation

Freedom of speech is not limited to political discourse; it also encompasses artistic expression, academic research, and scientific inquiry. Chilling effects in these domains can stifle creativity and innovation. When individuals are afraid to explore unconventional ideas or challenge established norms, society loses out on the potential breakthroughs that arise from pushing boundaries.

Navigating Cultural Sensitivities

1. Balancing Freedom and Responsibility

The clash between freedom of speech and cultural sensitivities is a complex challenge in diverse societies. While the right to express oneself is vital, it must also be balanced with an understanding of the impact words can have on marginalized or historically oppressed groups. Finding this balance requires thoughtful consideration of the potential harm caused by certain expressions.

2. Education and Dialogue

Promoting education and open dialogue can play a crucial role in addressing chilling effects related to cultural sensitivities. Encouraging conversations that acknowledge diverse perspectives and historical contexts can help individuals better navigate the nuances of expression while respecting the rights and feelings of others.

Overcoming Chilling Effects

1. Legal Protections and Advocacy

Legal protections are a cornerstone of preserving freedom of speech. Advocacy groups, journalists, and legal experts play a crucial role in defending individuals facing chilling effects. By challenging unconstitutional restrictions and shedding light on cases of self-censorship, these actors contribute to a more robust protection of expressive freedoms.

2. Fostering Inclusive Online Spaces

Online platforms have a responsibility to foster inclusive environments that encourage open expression. This can be achieved through transparent content moderation policies, user-friendly reporting mechanisms, and algorithmic transparency. Striking a balance between curbing hate speech and promoting diverse viewpoints can help mitigate chilling effects in digital spaces.

3. Cultivating a Culture of Respectful Debate

Society plays a role in mitigating chilling effects by cultivating a culture of respectful debate. Encouraging empathy, active listening, and constructive engagement can create an environment where individuals feel safe expressing dissenting opinions. When people are confident that their ideas will be met with thoughtful consideration rather than hostility, self-censorship is less likely to take hold.

Conclusion

Chilling effects represent a complex challenge to the cherished value of freedom of speech in our diverse world. As societies grapple with the tension between preserving individual rights and fostering inclusive environments, it's essential to recognize the multifaceted factors contributing to self-censorship. By addressing the psychological, technological, and societal dimensions of chilling effects, we can work toward a future where individuals feel empowered to express themselves without fear, contributing to a richer and more vibrant global discourse.

Introduction

In a rapidly evolving global society, the intersection of political correctness and freedom of speech has become a contentious and complex issue. While freedom of speech is a fundamental right cherished in democratic societies, the rise of political correctness has prompted important conversations about the boundaries of expression and the potential impact on marginalized communities. This chapter delves into the nuances of this relationship, examining the origins of political correctness, its objectives, challenges, and its impact on the broader concept of freedom of speech in today's diverse world.

The Genesis of Political Correctness

1. Defining Political Correctness

Political correctness (PC) emerged as a term in the mid-20th century, initially coined to describe adherence to a particular political ideology. Over time, the term evolved to encompass the use of language and behavior that aim to avoid offense or discrimination, particularly toward historically marginalized groups. Its intent was to foster inclusivity and sensitivity, but its implementation and effects are subject to ongoing debate.

2. Historical Context

The origins of political correctness can be traced back to social justice movements, including civil rights, feminism, and LGBTQ+ advocacy. These movements highlighted the need for language and behavior that respects the dignity and rights of all individuals. While noble in its intentions, political correctness has also been criticized for potentially stifling open discourse.

Objectives and Challenges

1. Promoting Inclusivity

One of the primary goals of political correctness is to create a more inclusive and equitable society by curbing language and actions that perpetuate stereotypes or marginalize certain groups. By encouraging respectful communication, proponents believe it can contribute to a safer and more respectful environment for everyone.

2. Navigating the Boundaries

However, navigating the boundaries of political correctness proves challenging. Determining what constitutes offensive language can be subjective and complex, varying across cultural contexts and individual perspectives. This leads to questions about whether PC measures inadvertently limit freedom of expression and stifle honest discussions.

3. The Paradox of Censorship

Critics argue that excessive political correctness can lead to a paradoxical situation where the drive to avoid causing offense inadvertently leads to censorship. When certain ideas or perspectives are deemed too controversial to discuss openly, it hinders the free exchange of thoughts and ideas essential for societal progress.

The Impact on Freedom of Speech

1. Freedom of Speech in Democracies

Freedom of speech is a cornerstone of democratic societies, allowing citizens to voice their opinions, challenge authority, and engage in healthy debates. However, the rise of political correctness has led to clashes between the pursuit of open discourse and the desire to prevent harm or discrimination.

2. Chilling Effects

Concerns over "chilling effects" on free speech have arisen due to the fear of backlash for expressing unpopular or dissenting views. Individuals may self-censor to avoid backlash, impacting the diversity of opinions in public discourse. This raises questions about whether the balance between promoting sensitivity and preserving freedom of speech is being maintained.

3. Institutional Impact

In some cases, political correctness has extended to institutional policies and regulations. Academic institutions, workplaces, and online platforms have implemented guidelines to curb offensive language, often leading to debates over whether these measures protect marginalized voices or stifle open debate.

Navigating a Diverse World

1. Cultural Sensitivity

In a world characterized by diverse cultures and perspectives, being culturally sensitive is vital. However, the challenge lies in recognizing that what might be politically correct in one context could be perceived differently elsewhere. Striking a balance between acknowledging cultural differences and avoiding a one-size-fits-all approach is crucial.

2. Education and Dialogue

Engaging in open dialogues about political correctness and its implications is essential. Education plays a pivotal role in helping individuals understand the nuances of language, history, and power dynamics, enabling them to engage in respectful conversations that bridge gaps between differing viewpoints.

3. Fostering Inclusive Spaces

Rather than relying solely on rigid rules, the focus could shift toward fostering environments where individuals willingly embrace sensitivity and inclusivity. Encouraging empathy and self-awareness can lead to more thoughtful speech without resorting to rigid censorship.

Conclusion

Political correctness and freedom of speech represent a complex interplay between the desire to create an inclusive society and the imperative to protect open discourse. Balancing these objectives is an ongoing challenge, particularly as society becomes more diverse and interconnected. The evolution of political correctness underscores the importance of ongoing dialogue, education, and an appreciation for the complexities of language and culture. In a world where perspectives are multifaceted, finding common ground while upholding the values of both political correctness and freedom of speech remains a

central task for individuals, institutions, and societies as a
whole.

Introduction

In the digital age, social media has emerged as a powerful platform that enables individuals to connect, share, and express their thoughts on a global scale. As a tool for communication and self-expression, social media has undoubtedly transformed the way we interact with one another and access information. However, the advent of social media has also introduced complex challenges to the fundamental right of freedom of speech. This chapter explores the intricate relationship between social media and freedom of speech, shedding light on the potential benefits and the nuanced challenges it poses in a diverse world.

The Promise of Social Media

1. Connecting a Global Audience

Social media platforms, such as Facebook, Twitter, Instagram, and YouTube, have enabled individuals to reach a global audience instantaneously. This interconnectedness has provided unprecedented opportunities for marginalized voices to be heard, often bypassing traditional gatekeepers and intermediaries.

2. Democratization of Information Sharing

The democratization of information sharing through social media has broken down barriers to entry for public discourse. Anyone with an internet connection can now participate in discussions, share their opinions, and contribute to the formation of public opinion.

3. Promoting Cultural Exchange and Understanding

Social media facilitates cross-cultural exchanges, enabling individuals from different backgrounds to engage in dialogue and foster understanding. This has the potential to bridge gaps and challenge stereotypes by exposing people to diverse perspectives and experiences.

Challenges to Freedom of Speech in the Digital Age

1. Echo Chambers and Polarization

While social media promises diversity of opinion, it has inadvertently given rise to echo chambers—spaces where users are exposed predominantly to ideas that align with their preexisting beliefs. This has led to increased polarization, as individuals become more entrenched in their viewpoints and less willing to engage with dissenting opinions.

2. Online Harassment and Hate Speech

The anonymity and distance provided by the online environment have contributed to a rise in online harassment and hate speech. Trolls and malicious actors exploit the medium to target individuals and groups based on their race, gender, religion, or other characteristics, creating an environment that stifles meaningful discourse.

3. Spread of Misinformation

The rapid dissemination of information on social media has enabled the spread of misinformation and fake news. False narratives can quickly gain traction, leading to public confusion and manipulation. This challenges the reliability of information sources and erodes trust in shared facts.

Moderation and Content Curation

1. The Dilemma of Moderation

Social media platforms face a complex dilemma when it comes to moderating content. On one hand, they strive to create safe online spaces by curbing hate speech, harassment, and harmful content. On the other hand, overzealous moderation can be seen as infringing on users' freedom of expression and imposing a specific ideological agenda.

2. Balancing Free Speech and Harm Prevention

Determining the line between protecting free speech and preventing harm is a constant challenge for social media companies. Deciding when to remove or label content that may incite violence or spread false information requires a delicate balance between maintaining an open platform and safeguarding users.

3. Algorithmic Influence on Content Exposure

The algorithms that determine which content users see on their social media feeds also play a significant role in shaping discourse. These algorithms are designed to maximize user engagement, often leading to the prioritization of sensational or polarizing content. This raises concerns about the potential for algorithmic echo chambers that reinforce existing biases.

Navigating Cultural Sensitivities and Global Norms

1. Cultural Relativism and Speech Norms

Social media transcends borders, but cultural norms and values regarding freedom of speech vary widely. What might be considered acceptable discourse in one culture could be deeply offensive in another. Platforms must grapple with finding a balance that respects cultural sensitivities while upholding a global standard for open expression.

2. The Challenge of Hate Speech Across Cultures

Hate speech takes on different forms in different cultures, further complicating content moderation efforts. What constitutes hate speech in one context might be deemed legitimate political expression in another. This challenge highlights the need for culturally competent moderation practices.

3. Addressing Language Barriers

Social media's global reach also brings to light the challenge of addressing content in multiple languages. The nuances of language and cultural context can be lost in translation, potentially leading to misinterpretations and misunderstandings that affect cross-cultural communication.

The Role of Regulation and Self-Governance

1. Calls for Regulation

As concerns about the negative impacts of social media on freedom of speech have grown, calls for regulation have become louder. Governments and international bodies are grappling with the need to strike a balance between protecting individuals from harm and ensuring open dialogue.

2. Platform Self-Governance

Social media platforms have implemented their own content guidelines and moderation policies. While self-governance empowers platforms to address issues swiftly, it also places an enormous responsibility on private entities to make decisions that have public implications.

3. Collaborative Solutions

Finding solutions to the challenges posed by social media requires collaboration between platforms, governments, civil society organizations, and users themselves. Multistakeholder approaches can lead to more comprehensive and balanced strategies that respect the complexities of the digital landscape.

Conclusion

Social media has revolutionized the way we communicate and exercise our right to freedom of speech. While it offers unprecedented opportunities for amplifying diverse voices and fostering global dialogue, it also presents intricate challenges that must be navigated thoughtfully. Striking a balance between safeguarding open expression and preventing harm requires a multifaceted approach involving platforms, regulators, and society at large. As we continue to navigate the evolving digital landscape, the challenge remains: How do we harness the potential of social media while upholding the principles of free speech in a diverse and interconnected world?

Introduction

In an increasingly interconnected and diverse world, the concept of freedom of speech stands as a fundamental pillar of democratic societies. This freedom allows individuals to express their thoughts, opinions, and ideas without fear of retribution, fostering open discourse and the exchange of ideas. However, this freedom is not without its challenges. One of the most significant challenges is censorship, a practice that involves the suppression or control of information, ideas, or artistic expression. This chapter explores the multifaceted threats and challenges that censorship poses to freedom of speech, delving into its historical context, forms, justifications, and potential consequences.

Historical Context of Censorship

Censorship is not a new phenomenon; its roots can be traced back to ancient civilizations. Various cultures and societies have employed censorship to control narratives, protect societal norms, and maintain power dynamics. From ancient Rome's banning of "dangerous" literature to medieval church authorities censoring heretical writings, examples of censorship abound throughout history. However, modern democracies emerged with a commitment to protecting freedom of speech as a counterbalance to the autocratic practices of the past.

Forms of Censorship

1. Government Censorship

One of the most recognized forms of censorship is government-imposed restrictions on speech. Governments may limit access to information, control media outlets, and suppress dissenting voices. This form of censorship can manifest through laws, regulations, and state-controlled media. Examples range from China's Great Firewall, which restricts citizens' access to foreign websites, to North Korea's tightly controlled media landscape.

2. Self-Censorship

Self-censorship occurs when individuals or groups voluntarily withhold their opinions or expressions due to fear of backlash, legal repercussions, or societal pressures. This phenomenon is often driven by concerns about personal safety, job security, or social ostracism. In environments where freedom of speech is not fully protected, self-censorship can significantly stifle open discourse and hinder the exchange of diverse ideas.

3. Corporate Censorship

In the digital age, technology companies and social media platforms have gained immense power over information dissemination. Corporate censorship refers to instances where these entities regulate or remove content based on their policies, often in response to public pressure or to avoid controversy. While companies may argue that such actions are necessary to maintain civil discourse, critics raise concerns about the concentration of power and the potential for suppressing dissenting voices.

Justifications for Censorship

1. Protection of Public Order and Morality

Governments and institutions often justify censorship by claiming it is necessary to maintain public order and uphold societal values. However, determining what constitutes "public order" or "morality" can be highly subjective and open to abuse. This justification can lead to the suppression of legitimate dissent and the imposition of one group's beliefs on a diverse society.

2. National Security

Censorship is sometimes invoked in the name of national security, particularly during times of conflict or perceived threats. While safeguarding a nation's security is crucial, this rationale can be exploited to silence critics and limit transparency. Balancing security concerns with the preservation of freedom of speech is a delicate task that requires careful consideration.

3. Hate Speech and Harmful Content

Efforts to combat hate speech and harmful content have led to debates about the boundaries of acceptable speech. While there is a consensus that certain forms of speech can incite violence or discrimination, defining the limits of acceptable expression is challenging. Striking the right balance between protecting marginalized groups and safeguarding free speech remains a contentious issue.

Consequences of Censorship

1. Suppression of Diversity and Creativity

Censorship can homogenize narratives and limit the diversity of voices and perspectives. When only a narrow range of ideas is permitted, marginalized or unconventional viewpoints are silenced. This stifles creativity and innovation, hindering societal progress and development.

2. Erosion of Trust and Transparency

Censorship can erode trust in institutions, particularly when information is manipulated or suppressed. In an era where disinformation spreads rapidly, transparency becomes crucial. When governments or corporations censor information, they risk being seen as untrustworthy actors, further contributing to a sense of skepticism and disillusionment.

3. Inhibition of Social Progress

The exchange of ideas, even controversial ones, is essential for social progress. Censoring ideas that challenge the status quo can hinder societal evolution. Movements advocating for civil rights, gender equality, and other transformative changes often depend on challenging prevailing norms and engaging in open debates.

4. Retreat from Democracy

Excessive censorship can pave the way for autocracy. When governments suppress dissenting voices, they undermine the democratic ideals of accountability and checks and balances. Over time, censorship can lead to a situation where a single perspective dominates and dissent is marginalized.

Navigating the Balance

1. Promoting Media Literacy

Media literacy education is crucial in helping individuals critically assess information and discern reliable sources from misinformation. By equipping citizens with the tools to analyze content, societies can empower individuals to make informed decisions and resist the influence of false narratives.

2. Clear Legal Frameworks

Robust legal frameworks that protect freedom of speech while also addressing potential harms can help strike a balance between competing interests. Laws should clearly define the limits of acceptable speech, distinguishing between legitimate criticism and harmful actions.

3. Protection of Whistleblowers

Whistleblowers play a vital role in uncovering misconduct and corruption. Safeguarding their ability to expose information without fear of retaliation is essential for maintaining accountability and transparency.

4. Diverse and Decentralized Platforms

Promoting a diverse range of platforms for expression can mitigate the impact of corporate censorship. Decentralized networks and platforms that are less susceptible to centralized control offer alternatives for individuals to share their ideas freely.

Conclusion

Censorship remains a complex and ongoing challenge to the fundamental right of freedom of speech. As societies become more interconnected and diverse, finding a balance between protecting individual expression and addressing potential harms becomes increasingly crucial. By promoting media literacy, enacting clear legal frameworks, protecting whistleblowers, and embracing diverse platforms, societies can strive to uphold the ideals of freedom of speech in a rapidly evolving world. Recognizing the potential consequences of unchecked censorship, individuals, institutions, and governments must work together to ensure that open discourse remains a cornerstone of democratic societies.

Introduction

In today's rapidly evolving digital landscape, the concept of freedom of speech faces new challenges and complexities. The proliferation of fake news and disinformation has sparked a global debate about the boundaries and consequences of this fundamental right. While freedom of speech is a cornerstone of democratic societies, the unchecked spread of false information raises concerns about its potential to undermine the very foundations of truth, public discourse, and social cohesion. This chapter delves into the multifaceted issue of fake news and disinformation, exploring its implications for freedom of speech in an increasingly diverse world.

The Rise of Fake News and Disinformation

1. Technological Advancements and Information Spread

The digital revolution has transformed the way information is produced, consumed, and disseminated. The advent of social media platforms and online news sources has democratized access to information, enabling anyone with an internet connection to share their perspectives. However, this democratization has also opened the floodgates for the rapid spread of unverified or deliberately fabricated information.

2. The Virality Factor

Social media platforms prioritize engagement and shareability, often leading to the amplification of sensationalist and emotionally charged content. As a result, false or misleading information that elicits strong emotional responses tends to go viral faster than verified and balanced reporting. This virality poses a significant challenge to the accuracy and credibility of information circulating in the digital sphere.

Implications for Freedom of Speech

1. Erosion of Trust and Credibility

The widespread dissemination of fake news erodes public trust in media, institutions, and even democratic processes. When citizens cannot distinguish between accurate and false information, the credibility of news outlets and authoritative sources diminishes. This erosion of trust has the potential to delegitimize not only media organizations but also the very notion of objective truth, undermining the foundation of informed public discourse.

2. Threats to Democratic Discourse

A healthy democracy relies on well-informed citizens engaging in meaningful discourse to make informed decisions. The prevalence of disinformation muddles the waters of public discourse, making it difficult to distinguish genuine perspectives from manufactured narratives. When false information influences public opinion and policy debates, the integrity of democratic decision-making is compromised.

3. Polarization and Social Divides

Fake news often reinforces existing biases and beliefs, deepening societal divisions. Echo chambers form as individuals are exposed to information that aligns with their preconceived notions, leading to a reinforcement of their viewpoints. This isolation from diverse perspectives can hinder empathy and compromise, further fracturing societies along ideological lines.

Balancing Freedom of Speech and Information Integrity

1. The Paradox of Regulation

Efforts to combat fake news and disinformation have led to debates about the appropriate role of regulation. While regulation can help mitigate the harmful effects of false information, it also raises concerns about potential encroachments on freedom of speech. Striking the right balance between curbing misinformation and upholding the right to express diverse opinions remains a complex challenge.

2. Fact-Checking and Media Literacy

Promoting media literacy and critical thinking skills is essential in the digital age. Educating individuals about how to discern credible sources, verify information, and recognize common tactics used in spreading disinformation can empower them to be more discerning consumers of information. Fact-checking initiatives by both media organizations and independent watchdogs play a vital role in correcting false narratives.

3. Responsibility of Tech Companies

Social media platforms have become the primary conduits for the dissemination of fake news. As such, these tech companies have a significant role to play in curbing the spread of misinformation. Stricter content moderation policies, algorithms designed to prioritize accuracy over virality, and collaboration with fact-checking organizations can contribute to a more responsible information ecosystem.

Global Perspectives and Challenges

1. Cultural Nuances in Defining Truth

Different cultures have varying perspectives on truth and the boundaries of acceptable speech. What might be considered disinformation in one context could be regarded as a legitimate expression of opinion in another. Addressing fake news requires sensitivity to these cultural nuances while upholding universal standards of accuracy and accountability.

2. Challenges in Authoritarian Regimes

In authoritarian regimes, the spread of fake news can serve as a tool for suppressing dissent and manipulating public perception. While tackling disinformation in such contexts is crucial, it is also fraught with risks, as these efforts can be weaponized to stifle legitimate opposition and infringe upon genuine freedom of expression.

Conclusion

The digital age has ushered in unprecedented challenges to the concept of freedom of speech. The surge of fake news and disinformation tests the limits of this fundamental right, exposing vulnerabilities in the fabric of democratic societies. While upholding freedom of speech is essential, it must be balanced with the responsibility to ensure the accuracy and integrity of information circulating in the public domain. Strengthening media literacy, encouraging ethical practices among tech companies, and fostering international collaboration are all critical steps in addressing the implications of fake news and disinformation on freedom of speech in our diverse world. As we navigate this complex landscape, it is imperative to remember that the vitality of democracy hinges on an informed and engaged citizenry.

Introduction

In a world marked by diversity of opinions, cultures, and ideologies, the concept of freedom of speech has become both a pillar of democratic societies and a contentious issue. The ability to express one's thoughts and ideas without fear of censorship or punishment is considered a fundamental human right. However, this freedom is not without its complexities and challenges. As societies become more interconnected, questions about the ethics of freedom of speech arise. How do we balance the right to express ourselves with the potential harm that certain speech may cause to individuals and communities? This chapter delves into the intricacies of the ethics surrounding freedom of speech, exploring both the rights individuals possess and the responsibilities that come with exercising this freedom.

The Foundation of Freedom of Speech

1. Historical Context and Importance

Freedom of speech has deep historical roots, often traced back to the Enlightenment era when thinkers like John Locke and Voltaire championed the idea that individuals have the inherent right to express their thoughts without interference from the state. The concept gained further traction with the advent of democratic societies, where open discourse and the exchange of ideas were deemed essential for the functioning of a just and informed society.

Many modern democratic countries enshrine the right to freedom of speech in their constitutions or legal frameworks. For instance, the First Amendment of the United States Constitution guarantees citizens the right to freedom of speech, emphasizing its vital role in fostering democracy and safeguarding individual autonomy. Similarly, international organizations like the United Nations have recognized freedom of expression as a fundamental human right under the Universal Declaration of Human Rights.

Balancing Rights and Responsibilities

1. The Paradox of Tolerance

A key ethical challenge arises when considering how to handle speech that promotes hatred, discrimination, or violence. Philosopher Karl Popper introduced the "paradox of tolerance," which highlights the dilemma of whether a tolerant society should tolerate intolerance. If a society tolerates speech that incites harm or discrimination against certain groups, it risks undermining the very principles that protect freedom of speech in the first place.

2. Harm Principle and Limits

To address the paradox of tolerance, the harm principle is often invoked. Coined by philosopher John Stuart Mill, this principle suggests that while individuals should have the right to express themselves freely, this right is not absolute and can be limited when speech poses a direct threat of harm to others. Determining the threshold of harm, however, remains a complex task, as it involves weighing potential harm against the preservation of free expression.

Cultural and Social Considerations

1. Cultural Relativism vs. Universal Values

The ethics of freedom of speech take on different dimensions across cultures. Cultural relativism argues that what constitutes acceptable speech varies across societies due to differing cultural norms and values. While cultural sensitivity is crucial, advocating for universal human rights principles challenges the idea that certain forms of speech should be excused simply due to cultural context.

2. Hate Speech and Marginalized Communities

Hate speech often targets marginalized communities and can have lasting psychological, emotional, and societal effects. Balancing the right to free expression with the need to protect vulnerable groups is a critical ethical concern. Striking a balance requires acknowledging the history of systemic oppression and recognizing that silencing hate speech can be an act of empowerment for those who have historically been silenced.

Responsibilities of Speakers and Platforms

1. Social Media and Online Speech

The digital age has ushered in new platforms for expression, enabling individuals to share their thoughts with a global audience instantaneously. However, this also raises questions about the responsibility of social media platforms to moderate and regulate content. Striking a balance between free expression and preventing the spread of misinformation, harassment, and hate speech presents a complex ethical challenge.

2. Responsibility of Speakers

While individuals have the right to express their opinions, they also bear a responsibility to ensure that their speech is truthful, respectful, and contributes positively to public discourse. A commitment to ethical communication entails engaging in constructive debates, avoiding ad hominem attacks, and respecting the dignity of others.

Educating for Ethical Expression

1. Promoting Media Literacy

To foster a society where freedom of speech is exercised ethically, media literacy education is crucial. Teaching individuals to critically evaluate information, discern credible sources, and recognize biased narratives equips them to engage in informed discussions and counter the spread of misinformation.

2. Encouraging Civil Discourse

Civil discourse forms the bedrock of a healthy democratic society. Encouraging respectful dialogue, active listening, and the exchange of ideas helps create an environment where differing opinions can be discussed without resorting to hostility. Universities, workplaces, and community organizations play a pivotal role in nurturing spaces for civil discourse.

Conclusion

The ethics of freedom of speech navigate the intricate balance between individual rights and societal responsibilities. As societies continue to evolve in the face of globalization and technological advancements, addressing the complexities of free expression becomes increasingly urgent. Striving for a world where individuals can express themselves freely while upholding the principles of respect, truthfulness, and empathy remains a shared goal. By recognizing the significance of both rights and responsibilities in the realm of speech, we can contribute to a diverse world where dialogue thrives, and the dignity of all individuals is upheld.

Chapter 15. The Role of Freedom of Speech in Democracy

Introduction

In today's rapidly evolving global landscape, the concept of freedom of speech has emerged as a cornerstone of modern democratic societies. As part of the book "Freedom of Speech in a Diverse World," this chapter delves into the crucial role that freedom of speech plays within democratic frameworks. Democracy, as a political system, relies on open dialogue, diverse opinions, and the free exchange of ideas. The protection and promotion of freedom of speech are not merely symbolic gestures; they are essential for fostering an informed and engaged citizenry, ensuring government accountability, and maintaining societal progress.

The Essence of Democracy

1. Dialogue and Debate

At the heart of democracy lies the idea that decisions affecting the collective should be made through informed consent. Freedom of speech provides a platform for individuals to engage in dialogue and debate, enabling the sharing of diverse viewpoints, insights, and experiences. This exchange serves as a catalyst for societal progress by challenging conventional wisdom, stimulating critical thinking, and fostering innovation. Democratic societies thrive on the synergy between differing perspectives, allowing for comprehensive problem-solving and policy formulation.

A functioning democracy depends on the active participation of its citizens. Freedom of speech ensures that individuals have access to a wide range of information, allowing them to make well-informed decisions. In a diverse world, where information flows from various sources, the ability to access, evaluate, and contribute to information is vital for citizens to engage meaningfully in the democratic process. The empowered citizenry that emerges from such access becomes a potent force for shaping the direction of a nation.

Accountability and Transparency

1. Checking Power

The media, often referred to as the "fourth estate," plays a pivotal role in ensuring government accountability. Freedom of speech empowers journalists to investigate and report on matters of public interest without fear of censorship or retribution. Through investigative journalism, media outlets act as watchdogs, holding elected officials and institutions accountable for their actions. This role reinforces the checks and balances essential for preventing the abuse of power within democratic systems.

2. Whistleblowers and Civic Engagement

Whistleblowers, protected by the principles of freedom of speech, have played a significant role in uncovering corruption, human rights abuses, and other unethical practices. Their revelations not only expose wrongdoing but also foster a culture of transparency and integrity. In a diverse world, where power dynamics can be complex, the ability of individuals to voice concerns without fear of persecution is crucial for maintaining the ethical foundation of democracy. Whistleblowers encourage civic engagement by highlighting issues that require public attention and response.

Challenges and Complexities

1. Censorship and Extremism

While freedom of speech is integral to democracy, its exercise is not without challenges. Striking a balance between the preservation of open dialogue and preventing harm poses a delicate dilemma. The rise of extremist ideologies and hate speech has prompted discussions about the boundaries of free expression. In a diverse world, where conflicting viewpoints abound, finding common ground on issues related to censorship and extremism tests the resilience of democratic ideals.

2. Disinformation and Digital Age

The digital age has brought about unprecedented opportunities for the dissemination of information. However, it has also given rise to the rapid spread of disinformation and misinformation. The challenge lies in preserving the freedom of speech while mitigating the potentially harmful effects of false information on public discourse. Democracies must navigate this complex terrain by promoting media literacy, fact-checking, and responsible online behavior to maintain the integrity of their information ecosystems.

Fostering Inclusive Dialogue

1. Respecting Cultural Pluralism

In a diverse world, freedom of speech takes on added significance as societies grapple with cultural pluralism. Different cultures and traditions have varying perspectives on what constitutes acceptable speech. Balancing the universal principles of freedom of expression with cultural sensitivities requires nuanced approaches that respect diverse norms and values. Striking this balance enables societies to harness the benefits of open dialogue while fostering inclusivity and mutual respect.

2. Promoting Constructive Conversations

Open dialogue within democratic societies should aim at productive outcomes. While diverse opinions are essential, fostering a culture of constructive conversations is equally important. Freedom of speech should encourage the exchange of ideas that lead to actionable solutions and promote social cohesion. Creating spaces for respectful debates, where participants listen actively and engage thoughtfully, contributes to the overall health of democratic discourse.

Conclusion

The role of freedom of speech in democracy is multifaceted and profound. It serves as a catalyst for progress, enabling the exchange of diverse viewpoints and fostering critical thinking. Moreover, freedom of speech ensures government accountability by allowing for robust media scrutiny and the protection of whistleblowers. Nonetheless, challenges persist, including the need to balance free expression with

preventing harm and addressing the complexities of
disinformation in the digital age.

Chapter 16. The Influence of Globalization on Freedom of Speech

Introduction

In today's interconnected world, the rapid advancement of technology and communication has led to a phenomenon known as globalization. This phenomenon has significantly transformed the way people interact, share ideas, and access information across geographical boundaries. One of the most critical aspects influenced by globalization is freedom of speech, a cornerstone of democratic societies. This chapter explores the complex relationship between globalization and freedom of speech, delving into both the opportunities and challenges that arise as the world becomes more interconnected.

The Global Village

1. Digital Communication Revolution

Globalization has facilitated the emergence of a digital communication revolution, effectively turning the world into a global village. The internet, social media, and other digital platforms have enabled individuals to communicate and share ideas instantaneously, transcending physical barriers. This interconnectedness has created an unprecedented platform for expressing diverse viewpoints and promoting dialogue on a global scale.

2. Amplification of Marginalized Voices

One of the significant positive impacts of globalization on freedom of speech is the amplification of marginalized voices. Previously silenced or underrepresented groups now have the means to share their perspectives with a global audience. Social media, in particular, has been instrumental in giving voice to individuals and communities that were previously excluded from mainstream discourse. This inclusivity has enriched public discourse by introducing a wider range of perspectives.

Challenges to Freedom of Speech in a Globalized World

1. Cultural Relativism and Censorship

While globalization has expanded the reach of free expression, it has also exposed cultural differences that can lead to clashes over the limits of freedom of speech. Cultural relativism, the idea that norms and values vary across cultures, can be invoked to justify censorship or restrictions on certain forms of expression. This challenge becomes particularly evident when Western notions of free speech clash with more conservative cultural norms, potentially leading to self-censorship or state-imposed limitations on speech.

2. The Threat of Digital Authoritarianism

Globalization has not only empowered individuals but also governments and entities to wield digital tools for surveillance and control. Some countries have capitalized on the global nature of the internet to monitor and suppress dissent. This has given rise to the concept of digital authoritarianism, where governments use technology to manipulate online spaces, curbing the free exchange of ideas and suppressing opposition. As a result, while globalization has expanded the potential for speech, it has also opened the door to new forms of censorship.

3. Spread of Misinformation and Echo Chambers

The rapid dissemination of information through global networks has also led to the proliferation of misinformation and the creation of echo chambers. While globalization provides a platform for diverse voices, it also allows false information to spread quickly. Additionally, individuals are more likely to be exposed to viewpoints that align with their existing beliefs, reinforcing these beliefs and limiting exposure to alternative perspectives. This phenomenon challenges the concept of a well-informed public, as individuals may be misled by inaccurate information or isolated within their ideological bubbles.

Balancing Globalized Expression and Societal Values

1. Jurisdictional Challenges in the Online Sphere

The borderless nature of the internet presents a unique challenge when it comes to regulating online speech. Determining which jurisdiction's laws apply to online content can be complex, as content created in one country can easily be accessed in another. This challenge is particularly pronounced when content in one jurisdiction is considered legal but offensive in another. Striking a balance between allowing global expression while respecting local sensitivities remains a contentious issue.

2. The Role of Tech Companies

Globalization has also thrust technology companies into the role of moderators and arbiters of free speech. Platforms like social media networks are now responsible for enforcing community guidelines and determining the limits of acceptable expression. This role comes with immense power and influence over public discourse, raising questions about transparency, accountability, and the potential for bias in content moderation decisions.

As the challenges of balancing free speech with cultural diversity and technological influence become more complex, there is a growing need for international frameworks to address these issues. Collaborative efforts could establish common principles for protecting freedom of speech while considering cultural nuances and addressing the transnational nature of digital communication. However, such efforts must navigate the complexities of differing legal systems, cultural norms, and political agendas.

Conclusion

The influence of globalization on freedom of speech is a multifaceted and dynamic phenomenon. While it has expanded the reach of free expression and empowered marginalized voices, it has also introduced new challenges related to censorship, misinformation, and cultural clashes. Striking the right balance between a globalized exchange of ideas and respecting diverse values requires careful consideration and collaboration among various stakeholders, including governments, tech companies, and civil society.

Introduction

The advent of the digital age has revolutionized the way we communicate, share information, and engage in public discourse. The internet has emerged as a powerful platform for individuals to exercise their freedom of speech, enabling them to express opinions, challenge established norms, and advocate for social and political change. However, this newfound freedom has also brought about complex challenges related to online activism and cybersecurity. This chapter explores the intricate relationship between freedom of speech, online activism, and the crucial need for cybersecurity measures in the modern digital landscape.

The Evolution of Freedom of Speech in the Digital Era

1. The Internet as a Catalyst for Expression

The internet has democratized communication, granting a voice to millions who were previously marginalized or silenced. Social media platforms, blogs, and online forums have become virtual town squares where diverse voices can be heard, allowing for a greater variety of perspectives to shape public discourse.

2. Challenges to Traditional Notions of Freedom of Speech

The digital era has forced a reevaluation of traditional concepts of freedom of speech. Online spaces operate differently from traditional public spaces, raising questions about moderation, hate speech, and the role of platform owners in regulating content. Balancing the principles of free expression with the need to prevent harm and misinformation presents a complex ethical dilemma.

The Rise of Online Activism

1. Empowerment Through Digital Advocacy

Online activism, also known as "cyberactivism," has become a powerful tool for advancing social and political causes. From the Arab Spring uprisings to contemporary climate change movements, the internet provides a platform for organizing, mobilizing, and amplifying the voices of activists worldwide.

2. Hashtag Campaigns and Viral Movements

Hashtags and viral challenges have transformed the landscape of online activism. Movements like #BlackLivesMatter, #MeToo, and #FridaysForFuture have harnessed the viral nature of social media to raise awareness and drive real-world change. However, the transient nature of online trends raises concerns about the sustainability of impact and the potential for superficial engagement.

Cybersecurity and the Protection of Digital Speech

1. The Vulnerabilities of Online Expression

The digital age has not only expanded the opportunities for free speech but has also exposed individuals to new vulnerabilities. Hacking, doxing (the act of publicly revealing or sharing private and personal information about an individual without their consent, often with malicious intent), and online harassment are just a few of the threats that individuals advocating for change online may face. As a result, safeguarding digital speech has become synonymous with ensuring the safety and security of activists.

2. Government Surveillance and Censorship

While the internet offers a global platform for expression, it also enables governments to monitor and suppress dissent. Mass surveillance and censorship practices pose a significant threat to freedom of speech in the digital age. Striking a balance between national security interests and individual rights remains a contentious issue.

Navigating the Ethics of Online Speech

1. The Paradox of Anonymity and Accountability

Anonymity online has both positive and negative implications for freedom of speech. It can empower individuals to speak out without fear of reprisal, but it can also enable toxic behavior and the spread of misinformation. Balancing anonymity with accountability is a central challenge in fostering healthy online discourse.

2. Content Moderation and Platform Responsibility

The role of social media platforms in moderating content is a topic of intense debate. While content moderation can prevent the dissemination of harmful and false information, it also raises concerns about bias, censorship, and the concentration of power in the hands of a few corporations.

Strengthening Cybersecurity for Digital Activism

1. Empowering Individuals with Digital Literacy

Promoting digital literacy is essential in equipping individuals with the tools to navigate the online landscape safely. Understanding how to identify phishing attempts, secure personal data, and verify sources are crucial skills for activists and general users alike.

2. Encrypted Communication and Online Privacy

End-to-end encryption and secure communication tools offer a way to protect sensitive information and shield activists from prying eyes. However, these tools also raise concerns among law enforcement agencies, who argue that encryption can hinder investigations into criminal activity.

Conclusion

The digital age has undeniably expanded the scope of freedom of speech, providing a platform for global activism and the exchange of diverse ideas. However, this newfound freedom is not without its challenges. Online activism brings with it a host of cybersecurity concerns that can endanger both individuals and the broader democratic process. Striking the right balance between free expression, cybersecurity, and ethical considerations is essential in ensuring that the digital age remains a realm where voices can be heard, ideas can be debated, and positive change can be fostered. As we navigate this complex landscape, it is imperative that we continue to uphold the principles of free speech while adapting to the evolving realities of the online world.

Chapter 18. Future Challenges and Prospects for Freedom of Speech

Introduction

The concept of freedom of speech has long been regarded as a cornerstone of democratic societies, allowing individuals to express their thoughts, opinions, and ideas without fear of censorship or persecution. In an increasingly diverse and interconnected world, the landscape of freedom of speech is undergoing significant shifts, presenting both opportunities and challenges for its future. This chapter explores the evolving nature of freedom of speech and examines the potential obstacles and prospects it faces in a diverse global context.

The Digital Age and Its Impacts on Freedom of Speech

1. The Rise of Online Platforms

The digital age has revolutionized the way information is shared, giving individuals unprecedented access to a global audience through various online platforms. Social media, blogging platforms, and video-sharing websites have empowered individuals to express themselves, fostering vibrant digital communities. However, this newfound freedom has also brought about new challenges, including the spread of misinformation, hate speech, and echo chambers.

2. Moderation and Censorship

The role of online platform moderators and content policies has become a central issue in the debate over freedom of speech. Platforms are faced with the difficult task of balancing free expression with the need to combat harmful content. The challenge lies in defining the boundaries of acceptable speech while avoiding overreach that might stifle legitimate discourse.

Navigating Cultural and Global Differences

1. Cultural Relativism and Universality

As the world becomes more interconnected, clashes between different cultural norms and values are inevitable. The concept of freedom of speech is not universally understood in the same way across cultures. While some societies prioritize individual expression, others emphasize communal harmony and collective well-being. Striking a balance between respecting cultural differences and upholding fundamental human rights presents a complex challenge.

2. The Role of International Law

International human rights frameworks provide a foundation for discussing freedom of speech on a global scale. However, interpreting and applying these frameworks can be challenging when cultural contexts differ widely. Addressing these challenges requires diplomatic efforts to reconcile diverse perspectives while upholding the core principles of freedom of speech.

Balancing Innovation and Responsibility

1. Artificial Intelligence and Deepfakes

Advances in artificial intelligence have enabled the creation of hyper-realistic manipulated media, commonly known as deepfakes. Deepfakes are manipulated digital media, typically videos or images, created using advanced machine learning techniques to convincingly replace or superimpose a person's likeness onto someone else's, often used for deceptive or misleading purposes. While these technologies hold potential for creative expression, they also raise concerns about the authenticity of information and the potential for their malicious use. Striking a balance between enabling innovation and preventing the spread of harmful misinformation is a critical challenge.

2. Protecting Political Discourse

In an era of polarized politics, safeguarding political discourse is paramount to maintaining a healthy democratic society. However, the rise of fake news and disinformation campaigns has eroded public trust in information sources. Balancing the need to counter false information without infringing upon free political expression is a delicate task.

The Evolving Notion of Privacy and Speech

1. Privacy in the Digital Age

The increasing amount of personal information shared online has led to a reevaluation of the boundaries between free speech and privacy. The right to express oneself should not infringe upon an individual's right to privacy, but defining where these boundaries lie can be complex. Striking a balance between the two rights requires careful consideration of the broader societal implications.

2. The Right to Be Forgotten

The "right to be forgotten" has emerged as a legal concept that allows individuals to request the removal of outdated or irrelevant information from search engine results. While this can enhance privacy, it also sparks debates about historical accuracy, public interest, and the potential for censorship. Finding a compromise that respects individual privacy without hindering access to important information is a pressing challenge.

Education and Media Literacy in the Digital Era

1. Nurturing Media Literacy

The proliferation of misinformation and disinformation highlights the need for robust media literacy education. Empowering individuals to critically evaluate sources and discern fact from fiction is essential for maintaining an informed citizenry. Incorporating media literacy into formal education systems and promoting it across all age groups is a pivotal step toward countering the challenges to freedom of speech posed by misinformation.

2. Addressing Digital Divides

As technology continues to advance, ensuring equitable access to digital platforms becomes crucial. Disparities in access to the internet and digital tools can further marginalize already vulnerable populations, limiting their ability to participate in online discourse. Bridging the digital divide is essential to fostering inclusive conversations and preserving freedom of speech for all.

Conclusion

The future of freedom of speech is at a crossroads, shaped by technological innovation, cultural diversity, and evolving societal norms. As we navigate these challenges, it is crucial to strike a balance between upholding the principles of free expression and addressing the potential harms that can arise. Embracing open dialogues, international cooperation, and education will be key in shaping a future where freedom of speech thrives in a diverse and interconnected world. By addressing the challenges head-on and capitalizing on the opportunities presented by new forms of communication, we can ensure that freedom of speech remains a fundamental pillar of democratic societies around the globe.

"Freedom of Speech in a Diverse World" is a comprehensive exploration of the intricate dynamics surrounding the vital concept of free expression in today's global society. This book delves into the historical underpinnings of freedom of speech laws and presents a contemporary understanding of its nuances. Each chapter thoughtfully dissects crucial themes, from the role of media and workplace dynamics to the intersection of culture, religion, and rights.

The book delves into the intricate balance between freedom of speech and hate speech, the challenges posed by censorship and fake news, and the ethical dimensions of this fundamental right. From navigating defamation boundaries to the impact of social media and political correctness, this book offers insightful analyses. It also investigates the interplay between freedom of speech and democracy, globalization's influence, and the unique challenges posed by the digital age. With an eye on the future, the book concludes by examining potential prospects and challenges. A must-read for those passionate about preserving and understanding the evolving landscape of free expression.

ABOUT THE AUTHOR

Mr. C. P. Kumar is a retired Scientist 'G' from National Institute of Hydrology, Roorkee, Uttarakhand, India. He is also a Reiki Healer and Chakra Balancing practitioner (with pendulum dowsing) and offers Emotional Freedom Technique (EFT) to help individuals with emotional issues. Mr. Kumar has authored many books on technical, spiritual, and social topics.

For further details, you may visit his webpage
https://www.angelfire.com/nh/cpkumar/virgo.html